THE WOMAN WHO COOKED HER HUSBAND

THE WOMAN WHO COOKED HER HUSBAND

by Debbie Isitt

JOSEF WEINBERGER PLAYS

LONDON

DEBBIE ISITT

Debbie Isitt trained as an actor at the Coventry Centre for the Performing Arts before touring Europe with the Cambridge Experimental Theatre Company. In 1986 she formed her highly acclaimed theatre company the Snarling Beasties and is still Artistic Director. Her plays have won several prestigious awards for the company including the Independent Theatre Award in 1989 for *Punch and Judy – the Real Story*, the Time Out Theatre Award for *Femme Fatale* and three consecutive seasons winning the Perrier Pick of the Fringe Award at the Edinburgh Fringe Festival, which in 1992 included *The Woman Who Cooked Her Husband*. She has also written *Matilda Liar!* which received a national UK tour in 1994 and *Johnny Watkins Walks on Water* for the Birmingham Repertory Theatre. In 1995 she was commissioned by BT to write the 1995 BT Biennial, and *Nasty Neighbours* subsequently entered the Guinness Book of World Records for the largest opening night in history – over 100 companies simultaneously presented the play throughout the UK and abroad.

As well as her work with the Snarling Beasties, Debbie has directed at the Belgrade Theatre, Coventry and her films include *The Lodger* for Channel Four, *Queer Kings* and *Nasty Neighbours*, which she also directed.

First published in 1993
by Josef Weinberger Ltd (pka Warner/Chappell Plays Ltd)
12-14 Mortimer Street, London, W1T 3JJ

ISBN 0 85676 163 X

The play is dedicated to my Mum and Dad

FOREWORD

The *Snarling Beasties Theatre Company* was set up by
Debbie Isitt and Mark Kilmurry in 1986 with the objective of
fusing text with a heightened theatrical style so that content
and visuals could be expressed together drawing influences
from European theatre and cinema.

THE WOMAN WHO COOKED HER HUSBAND, along with other
works by Isitt, works via a high-energy emotional journey.
Each character has its own route and the action flares when
the paths are crossed. Most of the work should be done out of
scene, building up the emotional truth ready to enter the
scene so that the actors can just "be" there during the scene.

The play should be served up at a fast, furious pace with
savage emotional input, clear fast thought changes and an
innocence that keeps the play alive and real.

The action is without props of any kind and the slick miming
of lighting cigarettes, pouring drinks, etc, should be crisp and
clear - not detracting from the realism but convincing the
audience there is a real cigarette, real drink, etc.

The action is contained in a small space with the actors
remaining on stage throughout but isolated by spotlights.
Lighting should be used to focus on the character's face as a
close-up in film, or open out to reveal sections of the stage as
"party" or "Hilary's house" - the more simple and sharp the
lighting, the more dramatic and cinematic the piece of work.

Dialogue exchanged with wit and passion, soliloquies played
with panache and flair but never completely hiding the pain
that runs very deep amongst all three characters.

THE WOMAN WHO COOKED HER HUSBAND is really a tragedy. It
has immense scope for a riotous evening, but the comedy
comes from truth. Identify the jealousy, the hurt, the anger,
the betrayal, the fear, the confusion, the triumph and have a
ball!

Debbie Isitt
1993

THE WOMAN WHO COOKED HER HUSBAND was produced by the Snarling Beasties Theatre Company as a co-production with the Arts Centre, University of Warwick, and first performed at the Arts Centre. In October, 1991, the production transferred to the Royal Court Theatre, London (upstairs). It was subsequently performed at the Assembly Rooms in Edinburgh as part of the 1992 Edinburgh Fringe Festival, and at the Purcell Rooms in London as part of the Pick of the Fringe season in October, 1992. The original cast was as follows:

HILARY	Beverly Klein
KENNETH	Mark Kilmurry
LAURA	Debbie Isitt

Directed by	Debbie Isitt
Designed by	Gary Tanner
Stage Managed by	Steve Kilmurry
Original music by	Junger and Parker

THE CHARACTERS

KENNETH is an ageing teddy boy. His costume is a green
taffeta drape coat with black drainpipe trousers.

HILARY is KENNETH's first wife. She is dressed in a green
taffeta outfit, green tights and shoes. She wears her hair in a
beehive.

LAURA is KENNETH's mistress. She is dressed in a green
taffeta dress, green tights and shoes. She wears her hair in a
beehive.

THE SETTING

The set is bottle green taffeta. Drapes as a backdrop, and a
raised platform - on it, a long dining table covered in the
same material. Three larger-than-life chairs covered, again,
in green taffeta. Steps down from the platform create a
downstage acting area. The dining table splits into two
halves, enabling the stage areas to be lit separately - one side
representing KENNETH and HILARY's house, the other side
KENNETH and LAURA's house. The table is pushed together for
the three "dinner scenes", when the three characters act
together.

The play is set somewhere near Liverpool, England, but
could be any working class town anywhere.

PROLOGUE

HILARY *lies across the dining table. She is lit by a single spotlight.*

HILARY   I first decided to cook my husband on the day
                he left me. The day he left me I cried for
                sixteen hours solid. When I looked in the
                mirror my face was all blotchy and I thought
                HE'S done this to you. HIM. Of course, when
                your husband leaves you the word BASTARD
                keeps coming into your head in big bold
                letters. At first it just forms silently on your
                lips. Then you start to mutter it under your
                breath, then you whisper it vehemently,
                spitting out the consonants and, as it drums in
                your head, so you bang it out deep and loud
                and it builds and it builds until, before you
                know it, you're screaming at the top of your
                voice, B A S T A R D !!!! When *your* husband
                leaves *you*, you'll know what I mean.

                (*A spotlight hits downstage centre.* KENNETH
                and LAURA *are waiting outside* HILARY'S *front
                door. She looks down at them.*)

                There's Bastard now. Bang on time as usual.
                The best thing I can say about him after
                nineteen years of marriage is that he's
                punctual. SHE'S come here too - HER - IT -
                they've come together for dinner - I suppose
                I'd better let them in.

                No, they can wait . . .

Scene One

Music: Rossini's "The Barber of Seville" Overture. Lights fade to black. They come up, as music fades, out on top of rostra with all three positioned around the table - KENNETH *in the middle, the women at either end.*

HILARY   So glad you decided to come - it makes a change from sitting here by myself - one doesn't like to cook for one - does one?

LAURA   I hope you haven't gone to too much trouble - we had a lot to eat for tea.

HILARY   So you're not hungry then!!!?

KENNETH   Of course we are - STARVING!

HILARY   Well I hope so. There's enough to feed the five thousand.

LAURA   Oh . . . well, smells good, Hilary.

HILARY   The proof of the pudding is in the eating.

LAURA   I'm on a diet.

HILARY   She doesn't need to diet, does she Kenneth?

KENNETH   No. She's beautiful the way she is . . .

HILARY   How lucky you are to have a husband who adores you, no matter what you look like. I haven't offered you a drink. What will it be - Kenneth?

KENNETH   The usual . . . er . . . white wine please.

HILARY   And you. What's your poison?

LAURA   I'll have what Ken has.

HILARY	How lovely! We're all having the same. There's a bottle cooling in kitchen. Won't be a sec, Lorraine.
LAURA	Laura.
HILARY	(*exiting to 'kitchen' area*) Whatever!
LAURA	(*to* KENNETH) Did we have to come tonight? I'm not in the mood for her, Ken.
KENNETH	Just keep smiling, Laura. Everything'll be alright.
HILARY	(*returning with drinks*) Everything alright?
	(*They both smile and nod.*)
LAURA	I'm getting face ache, Ken.
KENNETH	Well, relax then. Just be yourself.
LAURA	I can't be myself. She doesn't like me.
KENNETH	Of course she does.
LAURA	Look at the way she's staring at me.
KENNETH	You're imagining things.
LAURA	I feel sick.
KENNETH	You'll be alright.
LAURA	I will not be alright - it's not right coming here. It's not normal.
KENNETH	She's just trying to be friendly. Stop over-reacting, making a big deal out of everything.
LAURA	I don't make a big deal out of EVERYTHING - we should never have come. It's your fault - why can't you say no to her?

KENNETH   For God's sake, Laura, stop it!

HILARY   What's this? A lovers' tiff? We used to have
               them all the time, didn't we Kenneth - when
               we were lovers. (*In a whisper, to* KENNETH.) Is
               she always so miserable, Kenneth - so sulky?

KENNETH   Bit tired, that's all. She's been looking
               forward to coming, Hil. Needs a bit of
               cheering up.

HILARY   Really? She's not making much of an effort -
               if I didn't know better, I'd say she didn't
               want to be here.

KENNETH   No, no. She - we're - both thrilled you invited
               us - it's nice to behave in a civilised way, you
               know.

HILARY   After the way you treated me - still, I hope
               your wife feels the same. I wouldn't want to
               be the cause of any rift.

KENNETH   No - no - it's fine - everything's under
               control. You're looking very well - isn't
               Hilary looking well. Laura?

LAURA   Yes.

HILARY   Thank you - that's very kind. I always think
               when people tell me I look well they mean
               fat.

KENNETH   No.

LAURA   Yes.

HILARY   Well, I'm famished and I'd rather enjoy my
               food than my figure - Oh come on, sulky,
               cheer up.

LAURA   What does she mean, cheer up - what does she
               expect? What were you whispering about
               anyway?

KENNETH	When?
LAURA	Just then, you were talking about me.
KENNETH	Don't start getting paranoid. Hilary was only making a little joke.
LAURA	Well, there's no need to whisper - unless you were joking about me.
KENNETH	No - you don't know the person - someone we used to know.
LAURA	Oh, great. I didn't know you were going to discuss old times.
KENNETH	Shut up! What are we having for dinner, Hilary? Smells delicious.
HILARY	A very special dish, Kenneth - a surprise - that's what we're having for dinner - a surprise.
KENNETH	Well, knowing you, it will be extremely palatable.
HILARY	I hope so . . . you do both eat meat?
LAURA	Yes.
HILARY	Excellent! I couldn't bear it if you were vegetarians and I didn't think to ask Kenneth. I assumed you hadn't changed your taste in food, only women.
LAURA	She's staring at me again, Kenneth.
KENNETH	Don't be ridiculous. At least try and make an effort - she's been through a lot you know.
LAURA	And I haven't?!
KENNETH	Not now Laura, please!!!

LAURA

Why tonight? She knows it's special. Why invite us round tonight? And you have to say yes.

HILARY

(*interrupting*) I love to celebrate . . . any old reason will do for a little celebration - how long's it been?

KENNETH

Three years.

HILARY

Three years - my, my. Three whole years and still together - well done, both of you! How long did we last, Kenneth?

KENNETH

Nineteen.

HILARY

Is that all? Still, three years - you must be very pleased.

LAURA

Fucking thrilled.

KENNETH

Laura! Sorry, Hilary.

HILARY

Don't apologise for her - just let her be herself. A toast to the happy couple on their third wedding anniversary . . . Kenneth and . . . Laura . . . Cheers.

(LAURA *speaks her thoughts aloud but keeps looking at* KENNETH *and* HILARY.)

LAURA

She's so good at it, making me feel unwelcome and uncomfortable and I'm supposed to feel grateful because she's serving up dinner in our honour. See the way she looks at him - like she's hungry for him, after all these years - licking her lips, salivating. See the way she stares at me - smiling sweetly but behind those eyes, wicked thoughts. Look at them laughing together . . . (HILARY *and* KENNETH *laugh loudly then stop.*) . . . anyone would think they were still married, anyone would think it was their anniversary, their celebration - I should have brought them a present!

HILARY   Cigarette?

LAURA   I'll have one.

KENNETH   You don't smoke.

LAURA   So? I can have a cigarette if I want one.

HILARY   Oh dear, is she being a bit of a baby?

LAURA   No she isn't, she just fancies a smoke.

HILARY   Well, I've cigars if you'd rather, or a pipe.

LAURA   That doesn't surprise me, I can just see you with a pipe stuck in your gob.

KENNETH   Now Laura, we don't want any arguments.

LAURA   Nobody's arguing, Ken, just keep your nose out.

KENNETH   Can I help you with anything, Hilary?

HILARY   Not just now, everything's going according to plan.

LAURA   What is it you were going to do, Ken?

KENNETH   What!?

LAURA   How were you going to help?

KENNETH   I don't know - that would be up to Hilary.

LAURA   But you've never been in a kitchen before - how could you possibly help her?

KENNETH   Well, just so long as you don't go anywhere near it, we should all be safe from salmonella!

LAURA

Ken doesn't like my cooking Hilary - but he's always spoken very highly of yours . . .

HILARY

Well that's nice to know - we have to be appreciated for something.

LAURA

(*thinking aloud*) Yes, we do, and don't think I don't know what her game is - bringing him here, tempting him back with her fine food - showing me up for a fool . . . Well, I hope it burns and she serves up ashes, I hope it's souffle and it flops with a fart. Maybe I could sneak in there and turn up the oven - or better still, just turn it off so when she thinks it must be done, whatever it is, is uncooked and cold, still frozen in the middle - she'll have to send off for a take-away. And how disappointed he would be - so badly let down. I tried to stuff his face before we came so he wouldn't have an appetite but he sacrificed mine for hers - well, the fat pig might just regret it if there is no dinner at all. Besides - he only has to taste her trifle, sniff her soup, swallow her salmon mousse and he'll be in raptures - seventh heaven - I won't allow it - I won't tolerate it - I will not let him touch her food!!!

HILARY

Peanut, anyone?

LAURA

Ta!

HILARY

Perhaps I should put a record on . . . any requests? As if I didn't know what you'd like on, Kenneth!

LAURA

He's grown out of Elvis, if that's what you mean.

HILARY

Oh surely not! You haven't, have you?

KENNETH

You don't grow out of Elvis, Laura - you grow into him. (*To* HILARY.) She's never been able to appreciate the finer characteristics in

Presley's songs, though I've played them to
her in the hope that I'd persuade her of his
genius - there's none so deaf as those who
will not hear . . .

HILARY   You don't know what you're missing, Laura -
partying was always Kenneth's middle name,
when he danced, the room shook and the
records jumped - when he cracked a joke he
laughed louder than anybody else, and when
he'd had one too many, we all ran for cover -
his all-time hero was the King himself, Elvis
Aaron Presley - he never let anyone forget it,
not Kenneth, my husband!

(*The two women part the table for* KENNETH
who walks downstage through the middle as
"King Creole" plays.)

Scene Two

Flashback.

Spotlight hits KENNETH *downstage. He is entertaining at a*
party.

KENNETH   So there I was, doing 120 in the Saab, when
this bluebottle overtakes me - no sirens
flashing or nothing so I'm thinking bloody
cheek, laws for them are different to laws for
us - you know what I mean? So I put my foot
down didn't I? And me and this copper are
tearing down the M6 neck and neck at 150 -
then his tyre blew up before he could pull me
over! Ha! Can you get your breath? Pass us a
beer mate will ya? I've brought this bottle of
brandy with me - blow your head off it will -
absolutely beautiful - it's over there on the
table - go and try it Mickey - go on - you
won't get your breath, I'm telling you -
unbelievable - twenty eight quid a bottle - is
the food coming out - I'm starving - nice chili
wouldn't go amiss, eh? I'm sick of the sight

of sandwiches - went out for this meal the
other night - absolutely beautiful little place -
had this leg of lamb - this big - it was
unbelievable - that's the sort of portion you
should get - they haven't got a clue these
restaurants - little bit of this little bit of that -
wouldn't feed an insect - have you tried it
Mick? What do you think? Look at his face -
he's bright red! - What did I tell you? Knock
your head off your shoulders! Ha! Ha!
Beautiful stuff though if you drink it slow -
imported. We brought it back from Spain -
have you been? Beautiful country - once you
get out of the resorts the countryside goes on
for miles - toured half the country nearly -
stayed in some cracking little villas. Hilary
wasn't pleased - she wanted to stay in
Benidorm but that's a home from home isn't
it? If you're gonna go you might as well
explore the place - mind you they're mad
drivers them Spanish. We were on this coach
and he must have been doing 120, and their
roads aren't like ours, don't forget I mean, it
was bumpy bumpy all the way - Hilary was
scared to death - kept saying she was going to
be sick - God - wouldn't that have been lovely
- stink of sick for twelve hours on a coach -
Hello darling, I was just telling them about
Spain - they've been tasting the brandy - ha!
Ha! Anything to eat yet? And nobody's
dancing - they haven't got a clue have they?
We'll have to throw a party, Hil, show them
how it's done . . . had this fantastic barbecue
the other night - beautiful weather Sunday, it
was . . . pieces of chicken this big -
unbelievable . . .

(KENNETH *has been smoking a large cigar and*
drinking and sweating and getting more
unsteady on his feet as the speech progresses.
Cut to HILARY *standing next to* LAURA. *They*
obviously don't know each other so they
smoke and drink and smile and nod.)

HILARY	Are you on your own?
LAURA	Yeah - I've known Don and Sal for a few months but I don't know any of their friends.
HILARY	No boyfriend?
LAURA	He couldn't make it - and I'm not stopping in because of some fella.
HILARY	That's right - You go in there and enjoy yourself. Have a dance. I'm Hilary by the way.
LAURA	Laura - Are you with your husband, or . . . ?
HILARY	I'm afraid I am - he's in there somewhere - making a bloody fool of himself . . . I've been helping Sal with the food - there's not much here, but what there is we'll be bringing through in a minute - you'd better go and start and queue because my Kenneth'll have the lot.
LAURA	Do you want any help?
HILARY	No, you're alright - go on, go through.
LAURA	Thanks - see you later.

(Music: Elvis's "Surrender". LAURA makes her way down steps into the 'party' area. She dances on her own, looking for KENNETH. He spots her from the other side of the room and tries to get to her but is interrupted by people offering cigarettes, asking for lights, etc. He gets caught up in a 'conga' line and eventually pushes his way through the crowd and grabs LAURA around the waist. She is taken by surprise and tries to push him off. He turns her aggression into a dance routine that culminates with her head-butting him across the room. HILARY enters, with a tray of food. She speaks to LAURA and steps on KENNETH's chest to deposit the tray on a mimed table.)

HILARY   So you found him then? I was hoping you
            wouldn't. God, I'm so embarrassed - he's not
            always like this. Come on Kenneth, it's time
            to go.

KENNETH   No, not yet, I'm just starting to enjoy myself.

HILARY   You've always got to be the last to leave -
            frightened of missing something - you've had
            enough and I'm tired - please . . . how you
            getting home love? Shame, she's on her own.

LAURA   I'll get the bus - there's a late service.

HILARY   You will not - you can't be waiting at bus
            stops this time of night. You'll give Laura a
            lift, won't you Kenneth - drop me first, then
            take her home.

KENNETH   Yeah, yeah - of course - no problem - it's on
            the way - well a short diversion - won't take a
            minute - it would be my pleasure - any time -
            no trouble - I'd like to - really - it'd be great -
            just great.

HILARY   You see, he doesn't mind.

LAURA   I don't want to impose.

KENNETH   Impose?! Impose?! As if you would - it's a
            treat to have some company in the car - the
            times I've said to Hilary - what a lonely
            business driving is.

LAURA   I don't mind getting the bus.

HILARY   We wouldn't hear of it - you're not worried
            about him are you - take no notice - he's all
            talk, and he's used to driving pissed - you'll
            be alright.

KENNETH   I wouldn't dream of letting you slum it -
                 lovely woman like you - you deserve to travel
                 home in style.

HILARY   You've only got a Vauxhall Nova.

                 (KENNETH *looks round to see if anyone heard
                 his wife say that. His mood changes, he
                 becomes very annoyed.*)

KENNETH   Well it's better than the bus, isn't it? And
                 that's the discussion we were having -
                 whether she should go home by car or bus!

HILARY   I know the discussion we were having,
                 Kenneth - I started it. It was me who asked
                 her if she'd like a lift - I mean, left up to you
                 she'd be walking home.

KENNETH   I've just offered to drive her, haven't I?
                 You've just heard me say it haven't you!!?

HILARY   I can't think why she'd want to share a car
                 with such an arrogant pig as you I'm sure -
                 I'd rather take the bloody bus than ride with
                 you - you'll probably frighten her to death the
                 speed you drive - or worse have a smash and
                 both fly through the windscreen. If I were her
                 I'd walk - it's safer!

KENNETH   Well you're not her and no one's asking you
                 so shut your mouth and stop embarrassing the
                 poor girl.

HILARY   It's you embarrassing yourself with your
                 dancing and your talk of style - you ridiculous
                 man. Come on. I want to go home. Tara, Sal -
                 bugger's done it again! Yeah, keep the
                 brandy. See ya!

KENNETH   You what?

HILARY   Oh shut up - nobody liked it anyway. It's only fit for the plug hole. Hold him up love - let's get off.

              (*Both women pull him in opposite directions. Blackout. Lights up on* LAURA *and* KENNETH *in moonlight.*)

LAURA   You should have let me get the bus - it only caused an argument.

KENNETH   Don't be silly - I've told you, we always argue like that.

LAURA   Ken, I wish you'd tell her.

KENNETH   I will tell her, I will - just hang on that little bit longer.

LAURA   My nerves are on edge. I feel sick all the time.

KENNETH   Anyone would think we were committing a crime.

              (*Blackout.*)

Scene Three

Lights up on the morning after.

HILARY   Morning Kenneth.

KENNETH   Morning Hil.

HILARY   Want any breakfast?

KENNETH   Bacon and eggs.

HILARY   Leave us some money.

KENNETH   Sure babe, how much?

HILARY   Just to get dinner.

KENNETH   What are we having?

HILARY   Roast leg of lamb.

KENNETH   You know the way to my heart.

HILARY   Have a good day at work.

KENNETH   Will do.

HILARY   See you at five.

KENNETH   Bye now.

              (*The door slams. It slams again.*)

              Darling, I'm home.

HILARY   Did you have a good day?

KENNETH   I'm exhausted.

HILARY   Dinner's nearly ready.

KENNETH   Good, I'm starving.

HILARY   I've done your favourite.

KENNETH   Smells fantastic.

HILARY   There's a film on tonight.

KENNETH   Does it look any good?

HILARY   We could watch it in bed.

KENNETH   Sounds great.

HILARY   Ready to eat?

KENNETH   You know me.

HILARY   Come and get it!

              (*Beat.*)

              Morning Kenneth.

KENNETH   Morning Hil.

HILARY   Want any breakfast?

KENNETH   Just a piece of toast.

HILARY   Can I have some money?

KENNETH   Sure babe, how much?

HILARY   Just for some fags.

KENNETH   Is there food in for dinner?

HILARY   Spaghetti with meatballs.

KENNETH   Great - can't wait.

HILARY   Have a good day.

KENNETH   And you, my pet.

HILARY   See you at five.

KENNETH   'Bye now.

HILARY   Two teaspoons of salt and a sprinkling of
              garlic, pepper, tomatoes and meatballs - pasta
              and bread.

KENNETH   Darling - I'm home.

HILARY   You're looking tired.

KENNETH   You're looking great.

HILARY   Well take off your shoes.

KENNETH   Mmmm! Something smells good.

HILARY   Well it's not your feet.

KENNETH   What's wrong with my feet?

HILARY   Have you been running?

KENNETH   Don't be ridiculous - what do you mean?

HILARY   Don't take it to heart.

KENNETH   Well give it a rest.

HILARY   Give what a rest?

KENNETH   Your constant nagging.

HILARY   It was only a joke.

KENNETH   Well it wasn't funny.

HILARY   Spaghetti's ready.

KENNETH   I'm not very hungry.

HILARY   Morning Kenneth.

KENNETH   You haven't cooked breakfast.

HILARY   Did you sleep alright?

KENNETH   The sofa's hardly comfortable.

HILARY   It was your idea.

KENNETH   I'll do it myself.

HILARY   It won't take a minute.

KENNETH   You know I'll be late.

HILARY   Please let me do it.

KENNETH   Get out of my way.

HILARY   It'll be ready in a minute.

KENNETH   Some of us have to work for a living.

HILARY   See you at five.

(*Slam of door.*)

We haven't planned dinner - what shall I cook? He's left me no money - oh fuck.

(*Later.*)

HILARY   He could phone me - he knows how to use it - reverse the charges if he can't get change - he must have broken down - bloody car - bloody hell - where is he - I hope he hasn't had an accident - he has, he's had an accident and any minute the bluebottle will come to the door and . . . he's run out of petrol again - I wish he'd fix that gauge - you never know where you are with a faulty petrol gauge - maybe I should call the hospitals just in case - I can't send out a search party for a grown man - he's only two hours late from work - still he could ring, why wouldn't he ring - unless he's dead or injured - maybe he's nowhere near a call box - broken down on the 'A' road - trying to flag down help - if anything's happened to him I don't know what I'll do - I didn't say goodbye in a very nice voice this morning - I didn't even kiss him - and now I might never see his face again - Oh God - I should occupy my mind - read a book - watch some telly - I'm being silly, he's perfectly alright - something and nothing - we'll be laughing about it in an hour - if he isn't back by then I'll call the hospitals - I don't really know what to say to them and surely they'd ring me if he was in there - unless he's got no I.D. on him - they might be waiting for someone to call - and what if he's

in there all broken up - I don't think I could
stand it - best to just sit and wait - but I can't
bear to, just in case - I am - I'm being silly -
I'll count the cars as they come past the
window and if he isn't back by next week
then I'll phone . . .

(*Cut to* LAURA *and* KENNETH *having sex.*)

LAURA   Does she know you're here?

KENNETH   Who?

LAURA   Hilary, of course.

KENNETH   No, she doesn't know I'm here!!!

LAURA   Where are you supposed to be?

KENNETH   I haven't thought of anything yet.

LAURA   Well, why don't you ring her and tell her the
                truth?

KENNETH   No - she's not interested in where I am - she's
                all wrapped up in herself, there's no need.

LAURA   So you can stay the night then?

KENNETH   Oh no - no - I can't stay the night - I'd love to
                - but she's selfish like that - SHE doesn't
                want me but she'd hate anyone else to have
                me.

LAURA   Ken . . .

KENNETH   Yes . . .

LAURA   What was she like in bed?

KENNETH   Oh do you have to?!

LAURA   Tell me.

KENNETH   Very ordinary - very boring - she's not like
             you. She's only interested in cooking and
             cleaning.

LAURA   I can't understand women like that. I'd hate
             to be tied down to a house - I like to go out,
             have fun.

KENNETH   That's right - you don't know what it's been
             like for me - living with her. It's been like
             living with my mother.

LAURA   Well, don't go back there. Stay with me -
             phone her, tell her.

KENNETH   No - I can't - she hates phones - she won't
             answer them - she's got a phobia - a phone
             phobia - the ringing gives her a headache -
             it's best if I don't.

LAURA   Well, how long can you stay?

KENNETH   As soon as I've finished this - I'll have to go.

LAURA   Oh Ken why? She doesn't even care about you
             and I need you!

             (*They stop.*)

LAURA   Oh you haven't, have you?

KENNETH   I'm sorry - I couldn't help it.

LAURA   Oh it's not fair - the least you could do is try
             to make it last!

KENNETH   I'm sorry Laura - it's the stress I'm under -
             I'll make it up to you, I promise.

             (*They are still in a sexual position when they
             are interrupted by* HILARY *shouting.*)

HILARY   JESUS CHRIST! WHERE THE HELL HAVE
             YOU BEEN!!!? I'VE BEEN WORRIED

SICK!!! CAN'T YOU EVEN STICK YOUR
FINGERS IN THE DIAL AND PHONE?
BLOODY HELL, MY NERVES WON'T
STAND IT - WHERE THE HELL HAVE
YOU BEEN???????

(*Blackout.*)

Scene Four

*SUSPICION. The song "Suspicion" by Elvis starts as the
lights fade up on* KENNETH *and* HILARY *sitting at the table,*
KENNETH *holding out a cup while* HILARY *pours tea. They read
mimed newspapers.* KEN *kisses* HILARY *on her forehead to her
surprise. He makes his way down steps, takes his jacket off to
waist level and poses in a mirror, mimes putting on
aftershave and combing his quiff, etc. He looks at his fat
stomach in the mirror and tries to suck it in, when* HILARY
notices his back.

HILARY   What's that?

KENNETH   What?

HILARY   That scratch.

KENNETH   Where?

HILARY   All down your back.

                (*He looks at his back in the mirror and pulls
                jacket back on.*)

KENNETH   Nothing.

HILARY   What do you mean, nothing?

KENNETH   It's just a scratch.

HILARY   Well, how did you do it?

KENNETH   I don't know.

HILARY   You don't know?

KENNETH   No - I must have just scratched myself.

HILARY   How could you scratch yourself from the top
of your neck down to your backside - it's not
possible you can't have done it.

KENNETH   DON'T BLOODY TELL ME WHAT I CAN
AND CAN'T HAVE DONE - IF I SAY I DID
IT MYSELF THEN I DID IT MYSELF! ARE
YOU CRACKERS, WOMAN? I JUST USED
MY RIGHT HAND FOR THE TOP HALF
AND MY LEFT HAND FOR THE BOTTOM
HALF - I HAD AN ITCH - IT WAS AN
ACCIDENT - MY NAILS WERE SHARP -
YOU DON'T SPY ON ME AND TELL ME
WHAT I'VE DONE WHEN YOU KNOW
NOTHING ABOUT IT RIGHT! JUST STOP
HARASSING ME ALL THE TIME - I'M
WARNING YOU!!!

(The lights fade down on KENNETH *slyly
checking his scratch and* HILARY *slyly
checking* KEN. *In the blackout there are noises
of eating, dramatic slurping and chewing and
burping and slapping of lips and* KENNETH'S
*voice exclaiming "mmmmm" and "delicious"
and "tastes beautiful" and "I'm hungry - I'm
starving - I could eat a horse - mmmm!". The
lights come up on* KENNETH *and* LAURA. *He is
lying on top of her on the table munching her
earlobe.)*

KENNETH   My peaches and cream . . . milky white skin,
candy floss hair, cherry lips, juicy fruity . . .

*(*HILARY *appears in a surreal moment,
interrupting* KEN'S *antics. He is confused but
makes no attempt to move.)*

HILARY   Is it that I'm too fat, is that what it is?

KENNETH   No - no - honestly - I'm just very tired, you
             know all the overtime I've been putting in
             lately.

HILARY   I was wanting to ask you about that.

KENNETH   What?

HILARY   Well if you're doing so much overtime you
             should be picking up more money.

KENNETH   Eh - yeah, of course I am.

HILARY   Well, are you gonna start leaving more then?
             I mean, what are you spending it on?

KENNETH   I've - I've been putting it in the bank - save
             up to take you on holiday maybe - something
             like that.

HILARY   Oh well, that's nice. I'd like to go on holiday
             and could do with the rest. I know you've
             been working too hard - it's affecting your
             nerves.

KENNETH   It has - makes me jumpy - overtime - you're
             right - well - don't worry - I'll sort it out.

             (*Music - Rossini's "The Barber of Seville"
             Overture. All the action is mimed.* KENNETH'S
             attention shifts back to LAURA. *He looks at his
             watch and gestures that he has to go.* LAURA
             looks confused. KENNETH *slips away, blowing
             her kisses. She calls after him, annoyed.*
             KENNETH *leaps into centre spotlight,
             downstage, as though he has jumped onto a
             tube or bus. His right hand holds an
             imaginary strap above his head as he jigs
             about on the spot to the violent movement of
             the vehicle. It brakes dramatically and he
             bends forwards as it halts. He runs very fast
             up* HILARY'S *steps and greets her suspicion
             with a huge smile and sits at the table as she
             presents him with imaginary dinner. He lifts*

*lid of the dish and with exaggerated
appreciation he sniffs the air and makes
Italian gestures indicating "superb". He
proceeds to add salt and pepper, herbs,
spices, Parmesan cheese, ground pepper,
sauces, gravy and a cherry on top before
twisting spaghetti on fork and depositing it
into his mouth. He sucks in a spaghetti strand
and makes some "delicious" noises and
gestures. Suddenly he indicates that the food
is too hot and he needs a drink of water. He
runs back down the steps into the centre spot
for a shorter train journey, holding the strap
with the other hand to indicate going the
other way and runs quickly up* LAURA'S *steps.
As he reaches the top he breaks into slow
motion. Greeting* LAURA, *he mimes ripping off
his shirt and swinging it above his head,
throws it up in the air and glances at his
watch, sudden panic and catches the shirt on
the way down and pulls it on.* LAURA *cannot
believe he is going to escape again as he
apologetically makes his exit down the steps
and turns on the spot a la Charlie Chaplin
and up the* HILARY *steps out of breath and
sipping a glass of water he collapses into the
chair. Starts to eat the food very fast as the
music builds, slurps it off the plate, swigs
water, then he indicates to* HILARY *the need to
go to the toilet. He runs very fast down the
steps and straight up to* LAURA'S, *again
exploding into slow motion, he unbuttons his
flies letting trousers fall to ankles, looks at
watch and exclaims "Oh no!", as he pulls
trousers up and holding them at his waist he
jumps very fast down steps and jumps up*
HILARY'S *steps. Holding his arms out in a
"Hello, I'm back" gesture, his trousers fall to
the floor.* HILARY *looks shocked. Mouth open,
he looks down and pulls them up and runs out
of the house and back to* LAURA'S *and in a
slow motion finale, desperate, exhausted and
confused, strips off all his garments, throws
them around like a latin lover. He clambers*

onto the table and - with the last crescendo of the music - collapses behind the incredulous LAURA.)

LAURA   Where were you?

KENNETH   When?

LAURA   Last night! You promised me you'd come over - I waited in all night!

KENNETH   Oh - sorry! I got mixed up - it's very confusing. I haven't been sleeping.

LAURA   And what about me? Alone in my bed - I mean, what do you think? You're the only man in the world? I've got nothing better to do than wait around for you to show up? I have friends, you know - parties to go to, invitations I give up all the time for you - if you make an arrangement to see me then you bloody well turn up, alright! I'd done my hair, even tidied up - I must be mad. Now, are you coming round later or what?

(HILARY *is waiting for* KENNETH *to come in. She pounces on him as he's enveloped by a spotlight.*)

HILARY   Where have you been?

KENNETH   I've been for a drink.

HILARY   On your own?

KENNETH   Yes - why not?

HILARY   Where did you go?

KENNETH   Just to the Horseshoes.

HILARY   What did you drink?

KENNETH   Bitter - or was it gin - bitter, it was bitter.

HILARY   Who did you talk to?

KENNETH   No one.

                (*She walks down the steps and stands behind
                him in the spotlight, interrogating.*)

HILARY   What's that smell?

KENNETH   Smell? What sort of smell?

HILARY   Like aftershave.

KENNETH   It is - it's aftershave.

HILARY   Why are you wearing it?

KENNETH   Why not?

HILARY   You don't usually wear it - unless you go out.

KENNETH   I have been out.

HILARY   To the Horseshoes - on your own? Hardly a
                special occasion.

KENNETH   Just spur of the moment. I felt a bit smelly.

HILARY   Not nervous are you?

KENNETH   Why - why should I be nervous?

HILARY   How long did you stay?

KENNETH   About half an hour.

HILARY   Then where did you go?

KENNETH   Nowhere.

HILARY   Nowhere?

KENNETH   Nowhere.

HILARY   Are you sure?

KENNETH   Of course. Why do you ask?

HILARY   Just making conversation - will you be going
              out again tonight?

KENNETH   I shouldn't think so.

HILARY   Good.

KENNETH   Unless . . .

HILARY   Yes?

KENNETH   I might have to go and see Bob.

HILARY   Bob? Bob? Who's Bob?

KENNETH   Eh? My mate . . . he needs some help on his
              car.

HILARY   You don't know much about cars.

KENNETH   I can hold things for him - keep him company.

HILARY   You'll be wearing something old then to help
              on his car?

KENNETH   No need for that - he'll have a spare of
              overalls.

HILARY   Oh no you don't! I'm not washing and ironing
              unnecessarily - you can wear that old jumper
              and bell-bottomed jeans.

KENNETH   I can't wear those.

HILARY   Bob won't mind.

KENNETH   I mind.

HILARY   You don't need to impress Bob - he'll be
                wearing the same.

KENNETH   I can wear what I like!

HILARY   What would you like to wear?

KENNETH   Casual shirt and trousers - we might go for a
                drink once we've finished.

HILARY   On the car?

KENNETH   Dead right.

HILARY   Where?

KENNETH   Back to the Horseshoes.

HILARY   Right - I'll meet you in there.

KENNETH   Why? You don't like to come drinking with
                me and Bob.

HILARY   I would if you asked me.

KENNETH   I don't ask you because you don't like to.

HILARY   I'd like to tonight.

KENNETH   We might not go.

HILARY   You won't need clean clothes then.

KENNETH   But we might go.

HILARY   I'll see you in there then.

KENNETH   We're very spontaneous - me and Bob - if we
                go - we go, if we don't - we don't - we can't
                be worrying about what you're doing, Hilary.

HILARY   How long will it take?

KENNETH   What?

HILARY	The work on the car.
KENNETH	I don't know - could take some time.
HILARY	What's wrong with it then?
KENNETH	The suspension.
HILARY	The suspension?
KENNETH	Yes, that's what I said - now let me get on.
HILARY	Are you definitely going then?
KENNETH	Yes.
HILARY	Have you arranged it then?
KENNETH	Yes!!
HILARY	You said you might have to go out later - not that you'd definitely arranged it.
KENNETH	Well, definitely - probably - he's expecting me.
HILARY	What if I said I didn't want you to go and see Bob tonight?
KENNETH	Then I wouldn't see him.
HILARY	I don't want you to see him.
KENNETH	Why not? - What's the matter with you? It's arranged and I'm seeing him - why can't I see Bob - what have you got against him? He's a good mate of mine - why are you causing trouble - I'm seeing Bob, Hilary, whether you like it or not - he's my friend, good God, can't you understand I need men's company from time to time - do you have to be so selfish?!

HILARY   I didn't know he was so important to you . . .

KENNETH   Why do you have to make a big deal out of
                everything?

HILARY   It's not me who's making a big deal - it's not
                me whose squirming.

KENNETH   Squirming? Squirming? Why would I squirm?

HILARY   How the hell should I know?

                (HILARY *storms off to her chair.*)

KENNETH   You've got a screw loose, you have - you're
                losing your mind!! Just leave me alone - get
                off my back - go and get some professional
                help and don't talk to me until you're well!
                It's like living with a lunatic - you want to be
                careful. I'll have you certified!!

                (*Spotlight on* KENNETH.)

                She knows!!! I know she knows - I answered
                too quickly - "the suspension", I said straight
                off - I should have hesitated - maybe if I said
                something more convincing - like the fan belt
                - I don't know - how could she - we've been
                so discreet - my life's over - that's it - I'm
                finished! How could I have been so stupid? I
                should have told her straight - if you're
                implying something Hilary - just come out
                and say it - I assure you I've got nothing to
                hide - I should have laughed it off - said she
                has a warped sense of humour - but how could
                I - she never actually accused me of anything
                - it was indirect - cunning, but that's not like
                her - maybe she doesn't know - maybe I'm
                getting paranoid - course she doesn't - how
                could she? Oh, relief! It was just my
                conscience making me think - ha ha ha ha -
                but what if she does? We'll just have to be
                more careful - just in case - take extra
                precautions - I've had a bad scare, but there's

nothing she can prove - so relax - calm down,
in the future be more reassuring - be nicer to
her, buy some flowers - women and flowers,
the answer to all their fears - that's the sort of
stuff she needs - pay her more compliments -
not from the heart, Laura, just from the brain
- it's best all round if I tell her in my own
time - not let her find out - I can't stand the
thought all the screaming hysterics - all that
weeping and throwing plates, all the accusing
looks and hard done by speeches - we need to
be very, very secretive - what she don't know,
won't hurt her. Good, good, I feel better now.
The things I go through for you, I hope you
appreciate it.

(*A light appears on* LAURA.)

LAURA   I don't like telling lies - I'm not very good at
               it.

KENNETH   No, no, no. It's not telling lies exactly - it's
               more withholding the truth. This is our
               business, nothing to do with her - or anybody
               else for that matter - just keep it closed. It's
               not forever - just 'til the time is right to tell
               her.

LAURA   Well, I think you should tell her now. It's not
               fair on her, is it?

KENNETH   (*through gritted teeth*) I CAN'T tell her.

LAURA   Well I'll tell her.

KENNETH   I don't think so, Laura - she's not like you,
               she's different - neurotic.

LAURA   Well, get her pissed. She'll let it all out if she
               has a good session. It's not good for your
               nerves, bottling things up.

KENNETH   Finding out I'm having an affair won't be
               much good for her nerves.

LAURA	Oh. I'm an affair, am I? I thought I was a bit more important than that.
KENNETH	You are, you are - the truth is . . . she'd kill me.
LAURA	No she wouldn't, she loves you.
KENNETH	Do we have to talk about her at all - can't we just be together and forget she exists?
LAURA	I can't see how you're ever going to leave her if she doesn't exist.
KENNETH	When the time is right I'll tell her, but it might be better to put the split down to something else.
LAURA	Like what?
KENNETH	I don't know . . . money problems - differences - something that won't make her feel so angry and upset. You can understand that, can't you?
LAURA	No - if you're going to leave her she may as well know why. Anyway I hoped I might be friends with her once it's all finished. I haven't got any girlfriends to have a good natter with.
KENNETH	But Laura - she wouldn't . . . she won't . . . I think you're asking just a teeny, weeny bit much of her.
LAURA	You really underestimate the female, Ken. We're strong buggers, you know - she'll get over you, don't you worry and she'll probably need me to help her through it.
KENNETH	How can I put this? No, no, and no - just keep your bloody mouth shut and drop the subject.

If I find out you've told a living soul about us
you're gonna be in very big trouble.

(*Cut to* HILARY, *back at home, contemplating.*)

HILARY   Maybe it is me - maybe I am mental. I don't
want to feel like this - un-trusting and
suspicious. It feels horrible. But once the idea
comes into your head you have, you've got to
know. I'm sure I'm wrong - I hope I'm wrong
- of course I'm wrong but just to be sure I'll
plant a hair on his coat - I'll ask him how it
got there - watch his reaction - if he's cool
and disinterested then I've nothing to worry
about but if he's madly defensive then I think
I may have a problem.

(*She creeps over to him and plants a hair.*)

What's this? This isn't one of yours - it
certainly isn't mine - where did this come
from Kenneth?

KENNETH   How the bloody hell should I know you stupid
cow! What do you think I am, a mind reader?!
It could have come from anywhere - what are
you trying to say!!! It was probably a dog's or
something - Jesus! You're a spiteful bitch
with all your accusations - just get away from
me and get lost - leave me alone - can't you
see you're not well, it's driving me
nuts!!!!!!!!!!!!

HILARY   Have you been having an affair?

KENNETH   What?

HILARY   I want an honest answer. I hope the answer's
no, but if it's yes it doesn't mean the end of
our marriage, however, if you answer no and
the answer's yes and I find out you have lied
I'm gonna kill you. Are you having an affair?

(*Pause.*)

KENNETH   NO!! Of course not! How could you even
               think - I'm surprised at you! Very
               disappointed! No, no, definitely not! No!

               (*As* KENNETH *lies, so the lights fade out on
               them both, leaving his final "no" to be said in
               the dark. Music: Elvis's "Looking For
               Trouble" plays during blackout.*)

                        Scene Five

LAURA *turns up at* HILARY'S *to confront her with the truth.*

HILARY   Hello . . . I know you, don't I, it's . . . don't
               tell me . . .

LAURA   Laura.

HILARY   Laura, of course it is . . . what can I do for
               you? How did you know where I live?

LAURA   I've come for a chat.

HILARY   Oh, I suppose Sal told you it's an open house.
               Boyfriend trouble, is it?

LAURA   Yes it is, as a matter of fact. I don't really
               know how to tell you - I know you're going to
               kill me - I don't blame you - he won't tell you
               - I've begged him and begged him and I can't
               go on like this . . .

HILARY   Tell me what - who?

LAURA   You probably already know - I mean we met
               at one of Sal's parties - he was there - you
               couldn't make it . . .

HILARY   What dinner couldn't I make? What are you
               talking about? I go to all Sal's do's - she
               doesn't have a do if I don't go. Has she sent
               you about something?

LAURA	I've come to explain.
HILARY	Explain what?
LAURA	Why your husband's been so distant . . . Where he's been, what he's been up to.
HILARY	You what?
LAURA	He's been with me.
HILARY	Is this a joke, love - only I've got something burning under the grill . . .
LAURA	I just thought you ought to know.
HILARY	I don't know what you're talking about.
LAURA	I'm sorry.
HILARY	Yes, well, I'm sorry - I'm sorry, I can't think what you're on about. Whatever it is you've come here to say you'd better say it then piss off, I'm busy.
LAURA	Kenneth and I are lovers, we have been for a long time - he wouldn't tell you so I have.
	(*Pause.*)
HILARY	I'm sorry?
LAURA	I had to tell you.
HILARY	This isn't very funny.
LAURA	I know it isn't funny. I'm sorry, I had to tell you.
HILARY	There's a mistake - you're mixed up, you're telling lies - I'll tell my husband about you when he comes in - he won't take this lightly I can tell you . . . If you've got a grudge

against him for something, this is no way to
sort it out . . . I know you're lonely - on your
own - but just because you haven't got a
boyfriend you can't go round making up
stories, fantasizing about other women's
husbands . . . it was the party, wasn't it - you
were looking at me, jealous - because I had a
husband and you didn't.

LAURA   I honestly thought you knew . . . I mean you
must have known something. I suppose you
just didn't want to admit it. I think it's best if
you do. It is over, your marriage. Kenneth has
been planning to leave you for months.

HILARY   I've just about had enough of this . . . You
come to my house, tell me my marriage is
over - who the hell do you think you are? You
don't know my marriage, you haven't got a
clue what you're talking about - people like
you want locking up!

LAURA   It wasn't all my fault - I wasn't looking for
anything - it just happened. There must have
been something lacking.

HILARY   Is that right? Listen, if you're trying to tell
me my husband and I have a crap sex life
you're very much mistaken - if you're trying
to say my husband's told you we don't make
it any more, then you're a liar - even if my
husband knew who you were, he'd tell you
how much he loved me - and you to get lost -
all he needs he gets at home, don't worry
about that!

LAURA   He just doesn't fancy you any more.

HILARY   We've been married nearly twenty years -
nobody fancies each other after twenty years,
love - what the fuck is fancy? We make love
because we love each other. Are you thinking
of offering him a bit on the side, flattering his
ego? Try it, see where it gets you - I mean

anyone can do that - it doesn't make you special.

LAURA   I'm special enough that he wants to leave you for me.

HILARY   Leave me? You must be joking - you've completely imagined this whole thing. Kenneth wouldn't go with you if you were the last woman alive. I know his taste. I know him, I'm married to him - he loves this house - but of course you wouldn't know that, seeing as you don't know him . . .

LAURA   You'll get over it, I know you will.

HILARY   Get out.

LAURA   I'm sorry.

         (*Blackout. Music: "Looking For Trouble". Cut to* KENNETH *coming home from work. Lights rise as music fades.*)

KENNETH Hi Hilary - I'm home - what's cooking?

HILARY   Have you had a good day at work?

KENNETH Yep! What about you?

HILARY   I've had a great day.

KENNETH How come?

HILARY   No reason. I just had a really great day.

KENNETH What's for dinner? I'm starving.

HILARY   Nothing . . . I'll do you a salad.

KENNETH (*searching*) Where's my album?

HILARY   What album?

KENNETH   My *"Aloha Hawaii"* album.

HILARY   I don't know.

KENNETH   You don't know? Come on, you've spent the
               day tidying up, you must have moved it.

HILARY   I haven't touched it Kenneth.

KENNETH   Bloody hell!

HILARY   Did anything interesting happen to you today?

KENNETH   What do you mean, "interesting"? What sort
               of question is that? What are you getting at
               with your "interesting"?

HILARY   Nothing. I like to hear what you get up to.

KENNETH   What's "get up to"? Why would I want to "get
               up" to anything? It's work, a job - what's the
               matter with you?

HILARY   Nothing's the matter with me.

KENNETH   Always asking weird questions - why don't
               you just get off my back.

               (*Pause.*)

HILARY   Your album's in the bin.

KENNETH   What?

HILARY   I trod on it. It cracked - I threw it in the bin.

KENNETH   For God's sake, woman, that's my best
               record!

HILARY   You should have put it away.

KENNETH   What's wrong with you, can't you watch
               where you're putting your big feet?

HILARY	Yes.
KENNETH	On top of everything else now you're accident prone.
HILARY	It wasn't an accident.
KENNETH	You did it on purpose.
HILARY	Yes.
KENNETH	What do you mean?
HILARY	I trod on your stupid record on purpose.
KENNETH	You broke my record - on purpose!!?
HILARY	I JUST SAID SO, DIDN'T I?
KENNETH	You've got to be joking - people don't go around breaking my things for no reason.
HILARY	I'm not people, I'm your wife, and I had a good reason.
KENNETH	Why?
HILARY	I don't like it.
KENNETH	What?
HILARY	The record. It gets on my nerves.
KENNETH	You don't go around breaking other people's records just because they get on your nerves.
HILARY	I do.
KENNETH	Right. Give me the money.
HILARY	No.
KENNETH	Give me the money to buy a new one.

HILARY   No - get lost.

KENNETH   YOU are completely mental - I can't believe
              it.

HILARY   Why are you home so late?

KENNETH   The traffic was bad, why do you think? You
              break my record, you haven't cooked dinner,
              you give me the third degree on what I do
              every minute of the day - God knows why I
              married you.

              (*Pause.*)

HILARY   I saw Laura today.

              (*Pause. In the background, the Rossini
              Overture plays, indicating* KENNETH'S
              emotional panic.)

KENNETH   Who?

HILARY   Laura - you don't know her. Someone I met
              once at a party.

KENNETH   Oh yeah? What, like an old friend?

HILARY   Not really a friend. More an acquaintance.

KENNETH   Yeah? . . . And?

HILARY   Nothing.

KENNETH   Nothing?

HILARY   Nothing.

KENNETH   Fine.

HILARY   How long has it been going on?

KENNETH   What?

HILARY   How long?

KENNETH   I don't know what you're talking about.

HILARY   It could have been going on for years.

KENNETH   WHAT!?

HILARY   You could have been sleeping with me, eating with me, pretending to be faithful to me for years and years - you might at least let me know when it started.

KENNETH   Please, Hilary - I don't know what you mean.

                 (HILARY *begins pushing him out of her side of the house. He walks backwards, tripping up the steps, refusing to be forced out.*)

HILARY   Have there been any others? Come on, let's hear it, how many have you slipped it into?

KENNETH   Eh . . .

HILARY   Why, Kenneth? Is it my body that repulses you? My personality? The way I speak - what?

KENNETH   You're - you're . . . hysterical! You don't know what you're saying.

HILARY   Hysterical? I'm not hysterical . . . I want you out. Out of this house tonight - I want you to get out and stay out - you can pack a bag and that's all - you take nothing - do you hear - nothing - everything in this house is mine, it's mine - it's all I've got and I'm keeping it - you've got her - now go . . .

                 (*During the following dialogue - until the blackout - the Rossini Overture increases in volume until it drowns out their voices so we only see the hysteria as she shouts at him to go.*)

KENNETH   Go where?

HILARY   Now Kenneth - quick.

KENNETH   But I don't know what you mean? Have you been drinking?

HILARY   You're a very sad man - very sad.

KENNETH   You can't just throw me out on the street - what am I supposed to have done? You haven't even told me what I've done.

HILARY   Go!

KENNETH   If this is about Laura - I do know a Laura, but nothing's gone on between us - why won't you just talk to me? I hardly know her - there's no way I would have -

HILARY   Just - get - out - of - my - house.

KENNETH   You'll feel different tomorrow - I'll call round.

HILARY   How could you - how could you!?

              (*Split-second blackout. Music stops.* KENNETH *with* LAURA.)

KENNETH   HOW DARE YOU!? HOW DARE YOU!? YOU HAD NO RIGHT! Why didn't you just keep your mouth shut like I told you - then nobody would have got hurt.

LAURA   What about me?

KENNETH   Me! Me! Me! All you care about is yourself! Can't you see what you've done? She'll never recover from this, never! I'll have her on my conscience forever!

LAURA   She'll get over it.

KENNETH   Know her well, do you? I lived with her half
                 my life - we were very happily married. There
                 was nothing wrong with that marriage - why
                 did you have to go and spoil everything?

LAURA   You told me you wanted to leave her - you
                 told me you wanted to get married again - you
                 told me that marriage was over long before I
                 met you and now you tell me I've spoiled
                 everything!

KENNETH   I wanted to tell her when the time was right!

LAURA   The time was never going to be right! You
                 were lying to me and lying to her - it serves
                 you right!

KENNETH   I can't believe this - I've just been thrown out
                 of my house and I have to listen to this!!

LAURA   Go and tell her you want her back then.

KENNETH   I don't want her back!

LAURA   Well, she knows and that's that. It's better for
                 everyone to be out in the open. I didn't ask
                 for any of this - you called the shots. I've put
                 up with it longer than most would - sitting on
                 my own, waiting for you to phone, knowing
                 you're with her so don't blame me if it didn't
                 work out just like you planned. I mean, if all
                 you wanted was a bit on the side you should
                 have said - I would have contemplated it . . .
                 anyway, I think we should end this before
                 anyone else gets hurt.

KENNETH   WHAT! WHAT!!?

                 (*He puts his hands over his ears.*)

                 I can't believe I'm hearing this - no!!! What
                 are you saying? You're leaving me? I've just
                 left my wife for you and you're leaving me?

LAURA

Well if it was such a good marriage, I don't want to stand in your way - obviously your promises were empty.

KENNETH

No! No! They weren't - it's fine - everything's going to be great! I'm upset, that's all. Nineteen years, it's a long time . . .

(*Pause.*)

LAURA

So how did she take it?

KENNETH

She was very upset.

LAURA

She'll blame it on me.

KENNETH

Well, she'll come round - you'll see.

(*Lights up on* HILARY. *She is at the table chopping vegetables. Her mood had changed. The speech builds to rage.*)

HILARY

Not good enough for him? Not hot enough for him? Not young enough for him? HOW DARE HE THINK HE CAN DUMP ME - AFTER ALL THE COOKING I'VE DONE FOR HIM - I'll split open his head - I'll crack and rip and tear and split - I'll crunch him and chop him and cut him up and hack him to pieces - I'll slash his skin - I'll mince his flesh - I'll dissect and lacerate, tear him limb from limb - then carve him up - slice him nice and thin - the bastard - bastard - BASTARD!!!

(KENNETH *is standing at the door. He tries to escape.*)

KENNETH

I've just come for the rest of my things, but if your busy I'll . . .

HILARY

Well, you'd better come in.

KENNETH

Thanks - it won't take a minute.

(*He mimes getting his things together.*)

HILARY   What's it like . . . her place?

KENNETH   I'm staying with friends.

HILARY   LIAR! What is it she does for you? She must
              have something, my God - to throw all this
              away.

KENNETH   She makes me feel alive.

HILARY   What do you mean, alive?!

KENNETH   Virile - excited - alive.

HILARY   She makes your cock feel alive you mean!

KENNETH   Hilary, please don't be coarse - it doesn't suit
              you.

HILARY   And what does suit me, this fucking apron!

KENNETH   Oh God!

HILARY   That's it, hypocrite - turn to religion when
              you're in a bit of trouble.

KENNETH   Would you rather I didn't say anything - lied
              to you about her?

HILARY   Yes, dammit! Lie! It wouldn't kill you - tell
              me she's nothing - tell me I'm imagining
              things! Tell me it's me you love and no one
              else. LIE! LIE! LIE!

KENNETH   I can't.

HILARY   You lied to me at the alter - piece of piss -
              you said you'd love me forever - forsaking all
              others.

KENNETH   That was different.

HILARY   You're a born liar, Kenneth, but I told the truth when I said 'til death us do part - I MEANT IT!

(HILARY *mimes putting a knife at* KENNETH'S *throat*.)

KENNETH   Hilary, put it away - you're upset, you don't know what you're doing.

HILARY   I do know - I'm going to kill you.

KENNETH   It's just so unlike you - you're strong and together.

HILARY   We were together, you and me.

KENNETH   We still can be - I'll stop seeing her.

HILARY   See how the lies come pouring out now! Our whole life's been a lie.

KENNETH   I would have told you - I meant to - I didn't want to hurt you.

HILARY   Hurt me - is that what you think?

KENNETH   Well, obviously you're upset - I didn't want this.

HILARY   I bet you didn't! You wanted the best of both worlds! I know about men like you - I just didn't know you were one of them.

KENNETH   Can't we just talk?

HILARY   About what?

KENNETH   Anything - anything you want - tell me what to do.

HILARY   Why should I get you out of the little mess you're in?

KENNETH   I'll do anything you say.

HILARY   Because you're scared?

KENNETH   Because I love you.

HILARY   Love me? Apparently I killed you - I must
               have done if she makes you feel so alive, and
               if you're already dead it won't hurt if I kill
               you again will it?

KENNETH   For God's sake, Hilary!!

HILARY   Blasphemy! Adultery! You're the scum of the
               earth.

KENNETH   I'm sorry - I'm sorry - I think I should go.

HILARY   Go to hell - they're all waiting for you.

KENNETH   Please Hilary - you're over-reacting again!

               (*She pushes him to his knees.*)

HILARY   And what if I'd done it - Eh? Who'd be over-
               reacting if I got myself a toy boy?

KENNETH   You couldn't attract anyone now - you've lost
               all your looks - my life's not over yet - you're
               old, Hilary. I don't want to get old - I want to
               live the rest of my life like it's the first half
               over again - I'm sorry but you might as well
               know - you've become a fat old boring
               housewife and I don't want you any more.

               (*Pause.*)

HILARY   All those lies and finally the truth.

               (*She drops the knife. Cut to* LAURA *in
               spotlight. Music.*)

LAURA

So I'm a shrew and I'm a whore and I'm the villain of the piece and I was lonely and he was nice and I feel guilty and she feels sick and he feels angry that we can't just do what we want in life and I know how I'd feel if I was her and she was me but I don't know it wasn't planned - I didn't steal - I didn't know and once I did it was all too late and what do we do when we're caught up in the flow and we want to let go but we can't? So I hate myself and I love that sod and if I can just get her face out my head we'll be fine - well it's her problem really, not mine and I didn't tell her I'd love her forever he told her that and I wish it hadn't happened but it has and that's life and it's nobody's fault and everyone's hurt and soon we'll be dead so let's think of the starving in Africa and stop feeling sorry for ourselves!

(*Cut to* HILARY *in spotlight.*)

HILARY

Whispered lies - charming lies white lies and black lies - lies staring you in the face - lies told behind your back - deceived! Fool! Idiot! Can't you see through him he's taking you for the ride of your life don't fall for it dummy! My husband - the man I married - a liar, a hypocrite - making up stories - fabricating evidence - inventing friends called Bob!? How underhand can you get? What a shady, sanctimonious, smooth-tongued snide - how insidious - how sly - Mr Shifty nice and nifty left his wife approaching fifty who'd have thought he'd have so much guile behind that swindling bogus smile and me - outwitted, completely mystified by his trickery and collusion, months of confusion while all the time - well it all makes sense NOW - NOW I see as clear as the glass I'd like to smash over his head. NOW I know what it's all been about - it all falls very neatly into place, the horrible little man.

(*Cut to* KENNETH *in spotlight.*)

KENNETH   It's just so small - so squashed - I need some
space - the walls are coming in at me - I need
to move - to swing - it's all cramped up and
terraced - I need to get out - move up and on
expand - have scope and range - spread
myself - stretch my skin - elbow room and
freedom - I'm a big man! All these houses
exactly the same, different curtains - same
humdrum lives - it's boring - it's petty - it's
tiny and I'm suffocating - you are my escape
route - my ticket to the top - with you I'm a
new man with endless opportunities - energy
and optimism - I never thought I'd feel this
way I was beginning to think I'd been thrown
on the tip - like it was time I faced facts and
retired to a life of memories and old times
and look forward to dying and it scares me,
what's out there? None of us know but I don't
really have to think about it now - I can put it
off for a good few years, I'm starting again
and I feel just like a teenager.

(*Blackout.*)

Scene Six

Lights rise on LAURA'S *side.*

LAURA   How was she?

KENNETH   She was fine.

LAURA   There, I told you it would be alright - you
worry too much.

KENNETH   I need something to eat.

LAURA   Well do yourself a sandwich.

KENNETH   Do MYSELF a sandwich!!

LAURA   Yes - why not?

KENNETH   Because I don't want a bloody sandwich - I want a decent meal - you're starving me to death!

LAURA   Well you know where the kitchen is.

KENNETH   Yes, I know where it is, I just don't want to go in there - you're going to be my wife! Can't you even cook me a simple meal? Is that too much to ask?!

LAURA   You know I can't cook.

KENNETH   Of course you can cook - you're a bloody woman, aren't you? Hilary was right - you're a useless good for nothing child - nothing but a spoilt brat. You're no match for her.

LAURA   Well, get back there then if you miss her so much - and I don't give two shits what Hilary says about me, just 'cause she's bloody super wife - I'm not like that, so tough shit!

KENNETH   You might at least try!

LAURA   On your bike mate - go on, out! I'm not going to look after you just so you can shack up with somebody else when you need some excitement.

KENNETH   Well maybe I made a mistake . . .

LAURA   Yeah, maybe you did. And what are you going to do about it?

KENNETH   I don't know.

LAURA   Well, I'll tell you - you can clear out and you needn't bother coming back here unless you've got a big apology ready, right! And you can tell your ex-wife to mind her own business unless she wants me to go round and

tell her some home truths, tell her what her
precious Kenneth thought of her for nineteen
years of marriage, how he suffered at the
hands of a drudge and a nag and a frigid old
bag - how would you like that!

KENNETH   You wouldn't dare.

LAURA   Come on - don't kid yourself. I'm not
frightened of her or you!

KENNETH   Well alright, I'll make myself a sandwich . . .
don't worry about the meals, I'll sort them
out . . . please don't go and see her - I don't
want you getting upset.

LAURA   I'm already upset Ken - I don't want you
seeing her any more - I want you to forget
you ever met her.

          (HILARY, *in spotlight, talks to* KENNETH *while
          he's in* LAURA'S *house. Music: Elvis's "Love
          Letters" plays under speech.*)

HILARY   She threw herself at you - that's what it was.
Home wrecker! Marriage breaker! They're out
there - everywhere - swaying their hips,
smiling their secret smiles and how are you
Kenneth, now you're with her? Happy?
Fulfilled? Do you laugh together and cry
together and share together - take photies of
each other - send cards and gifts and flowers -
talk baby talk on the telephone - rush home
from work to be together, have hot baths and
rampant sex - late night drinks and breakfast
in towelling robes - his and hers - hers and his
- so she can't cook - to hell with it - eat out -
romantic restaurants - or chinese takeaway in
front of the telly - chopsticks not forks and
spill your rice and giggle and leave it 'til the
morning - leaving time for the love and the
lust and the fun and the things you've decided
matter *now* - when I always did.

KENNETH   It's not like that.

HILARY   Oh yes! She's got a waist - I know that's why
                 you went for her - she's got a waist and I
                 haven't, she's got a shape, not a trunk - with
                 tree trunk legs - she's got tiny bosoms not
                 mammoth mammary glands - she's called
                 Laura, all pretty and feminine, not Hilary all
                 dumpy and fat - what's she got that I haven't
                 got. You! She's got you!

KENNETH   But she's got disgusting habits. She leaves her
                 toenails to rot in the shag pile carpet. She
                 picks her scabs, she swears - she hasn't the
                 same . . . stature - in the community. I really
                 respect you, Hilary. I just love her.

HILARY   Oh that's alright then. I'll tell you where all
                 my pillar of the community spirit has got me -
                 my good manners, my clean habits - nowhere!
                 Left alone, with nothing to show for years of
                 trying to be a good wife.

KENNETH   Well - that kitchen has always been spotless.
                 You should be proud of that.

HILARY   Proud of a clean kitchen - my God, Kenneth -
                 after all we've been through - you leave me
                 with that.

KENNETH   Well, it's something to hold on to.

HILARY   Oh go on - go to her - your lovely - smelly -
                 dirty - sexy - lover - go and have deep throat
                 sex and leave me here in my sparkling
                 kitchen!!

KENNETH   Hey - I'll call round next week - keep your
                 chin up.

                 (HILARY *has moved downstage to her own
                 space, in spotlight.*)

HILARY   Hilary - once married to Kenneth - once
                attractive vivacious - virile - Hilary - once
                wife - woman of the world - of the home - the
                home being the world - Hilary - ex-wife -
                divorcee - dishevelled - dishonourable -
                Hilary - how are you? You're looking well!
                Hilary - are you sleeping at night - poor cow -
                Hilary, how is he - do you ever see him? -
                Hilary what of her - how can you stand it?
                Hilary where did you go wrong - Hilary - it
                wasn't your fault - Hilary come out with us -
                Hilary can I get you anything? - Hilary pull
                yourself together - oh Hilary - not crying
                again - Hilary he'll be back - Hilary forget
                him - Hilary men they're all the same Hilary
                Hilary Hilary! When are you going to wake
                up - you're not the girl you were - saw Ken
                today he's looking younger - getting on with
                his life - I hear they're getting married - will
                you go - what you need is another fella -
                someone to cheer you up - come on Hilary
                give it a rest - it's all been over a long time
                ago - can't you think of anything else - piss
                off Hilary you're boring us to tears, you're
                not the only one you know - so it was
                nineteen years - it's in the past - look to the
                future - Hilary for God's sake he's not coming
                back - and if he did - would you want him
                now? He's not coming back - he's not coming
                back.

                (*Cut to* LAURA *and* KENNETH. KENNETH *is
                asleep and wrapped around* LAURA, *snoring.
                They stand in the centre spotlight.*)

LAURA   Look at you, you smug pig. I feel sorry for
                you, I do - being the centre of attention - the
                focus for devotion - being cleaned for and
                cooked for and when you've had enough of
                one you start up with another - look at you -
                with your hair thinning and your jaw slacking
                - your belly potting - your gut belching - your
                arse farting and your feet stinking - who do
                you think you're fooling! You're not fooling

me! You're spreading into middle age like a
lump of lard gone soft - you'll never be happy
. . . never, 'cause you're a coward and a hoax
and if I had any sense in my little red head,
I'd see through your sham and you'd be out!
Not two wives but no wife and too old to
score and if you're wanting some nookie
you'll have to put your hand in your pocket
and pay up! Imagine that - after all the free
sex you've had that would hurt you Kenneth,
you tight-fisted sod! So if it's true and your
dick does have a life of it's own you'll have a
very expensive account at the local brothel
where I hope you catch something very nasty
and the fucking thing falls off!

KENNETH   Hilary, shut up.

(LAURA *looks surprised. Blackout.*)

Scene Seven

Music: Rossini's "Barber of Seville" Overture. Lights rise on
KENNETH *and* LAURA *at* HILARY'S *dinner table.*

LAURA   What's keeping her?

KENNETH   She doesn't just throw things together you
               know, Laura - she'll be doing all the business.

LAURA   Well, it'll be time to go to bed by the time we
               eat.

KENNETH   If you're bored you could always go home.

LAURA   You what?

KENNETH   Call a taxi and go home.

LAURA   And leave you here with your ex-wife?

KENNETH   Why not? What's wrong with that?

LAURA	It's our bloody wedding anniversary!!
KENNETH	Alright. Alright. No need to shout.
HILARY	(*interrupting*) Dinner shouldn't be much longer . . . any minute now.
KENNETH	Shall I put another record on?
HILARY	Why not? What about a dance? After all, it's supposed to be a celebration - go on, the two of you.
LAURA	I don't feel like dancing.
HILARY	Well come on then, Kenneth - me and you, for old time's sake . . . I don't suppose he's told you how we met?
LAURA	No - I've never asked.
HILARY	Tower Ballroom - remember?
	(*Music: "Stardust Melody". HILARY and KENNETH dance together, now transformed back to the Tower Ballroom. A glitter ball lights up the stage. LAURA, KENNETH and HILARY all react to the lighting change as a surreal happening. HILARY and KENNETH walk down opposite steps and meet down stage, talking to each other and taking in the audience, leaving LAURA watching in disgust.*)
	He looked at me from across the room and my heart started beating as if for the first time.
KENNETH	And then she smiled and nodded so I smiled back. I offered to buy her a drink.
HILARY	But I shook my head and indicated I'd had enough. He gestured, "do you wanna go?"

KENNETH   And she said, "no" - she had some friends
                 with her I think, so I said "how about the last
                 dance?"

HILARY   And I thought, "the last dance" - yes I'll save
                 it for him.

KENNETH   So she nodded "ok".

HILARY   And when they played *"Stardust Melody"* we
                 found each other in the crowd.

KENNETH   And I held her tight.

HILARY   And I held him tight - and he looked
                 handsome.

KENNETH   And she looked alright.

HILARY   And we danced and we kissed all through the
                 night.

                 (HILARY *and* KENNETH *spin round and are
                 about to kiss when the glitter ball cuts out.*
                 LAURA *bangs her fist on the record player,
                 causing it to scratch and stop abruptly.*)

LAURA   I think I'm going to throw up.

KENNETH   Not now Laura, please!

HILARY   It must be because of waiting for food - I'll
                 pop in and check - it won't be a mo . . . (*She
                 exits.*)

LAURA   I don't want her food. I want us to leave.

KENNETH   We can't leave - it's rude and besides which
                 I'm starving!

LAURA   You and your stomach, it's all you ever think
                 about!

(*Cut to* HILARY *who is singing "Stardust Melody". She notices the audience and stops, as if taken by surprise. She stands behind the table. To the audience.*)

HILARY

The kitchen is a murderer's paradise. Saucepans crack, knives chop, scissors stab, matches burn, microwaves electrocute, kettles of boiling water scald - the possibilities are endless - especially when you have an axe to grind.

It's funny really - considering we spend most of the time in the kitchen - why it is male murderers often want to cook their victims - I'm surprised they know how. But me - I'm an expert cook. I can disguise anything - the times I've served up yesterday's remains and with a little bit of this and a little bit of that - called it by a French name and fooled my husband into thinking he was eating something truly fresh and exotic. Well, food - like sex - is all in the mind.

Kenneth went to great lengths to encourage my interest in everything culinary. Well naturally, husbands want their wives to be good and careful cooks - their very health depends upon it. But how foolishly they trust, these men - how lacking in suspicion. How many wives have pondered poison while stirring in the gravy, then backing down at the last minute, just spat in it instead - It's food for thought though, isn't it?

It has taken me a long time to discover that even though I'm single and have been for many years, I'm still not free. I am suffering from the ex-wife syndrome, a bleak vision of the future has overtaken me - an image of myself growing old, alone, loving no one ever again. I am plagued by fantasies of him making love to her - still, now - I'm upset that he looks good, been able to move on with his life, because, when I look at myself in the mirror, I see an image of a woman who doesn't measure up, one who has been banished to the sidelines and replaced. I see nothing more than Kenneth's ex-wife.

Since the day he left me, obsessive thoughts have been slipping in and out of my mind, shocking, morbid ideas. That day, I was mincing some meat for my dinner and I had a spark - what would it be like to mince his flesh - would he make a good steak or a better spaghetti bolognaise - he's such a beefy man - not just skin and bone - he's really meaty - I can just smell the garlic on his breath - it's enough to frighten anyone to death.

(*Lights fade to black as "Stardust Melody" plays.*)

Scene Eight

Lights up on LAURA *and* KENNETH. *She thinks aloud. He, unaware, looks discontented and troubled.*

LAURA   Look at him sitting there dissatisfied, frustrated, uncompromising, afraid of nothing but death, yet killing himself with tension, stress, greed, booze and bloody-mindedness. We feed him, we create him, we allow him and we have no one but ourselves to blame when we find ourselves stuck with him.

He was married to her for a long time - he's bound to call her name out now and again when he's asleep or having sex. I don't mind that. I'll cook him something special, surprise him, get it just right, so tasty it will knock his socks off. He'll say, "Even Hilary couldn't have managed that". "Delicious", he'll say and smack his lips and ask for more - bloody hell, seconds! That'd be a first! We'll crack open a bottle and chink our glasses and he'll

look at me all proud and full, stuffed and
contented - he made the right choice. I'll even
clean up the place - well, you've got to work
at your marriage if you want your marriage to
work. I just can't seem to find the energy for
things like that, but I'll cook him something
edible if it's the last thing I do.

(*to* KEN) Dinner won't be a minute, love.

KENNETH   Why is this place always such a tip?

LAURA   I'm sorry, Ken. I'll do it again.

KENNETH   It's too bloody late now - I'm home - I'm here
               - I want it done before I get in from work,
               not have you dusting round me while I'm
               trying to relax. What the hell have you been
               doing all day?

LAURA   I've been cooking.

KENNETH   All bloody day?

LAURA   I've been shopping for it, preparing it - it's
               something special.

KENNETH   Well I'm not hungry.

LAURA   Not hungry - Ken, you must be - you haven't
               eaten.

KENNETH   I'm not in the mood for one of your efforts.

LAURA   Oh come on, you might at least try it, it's
               special!

KENNETH   If it's so bloody special, eat it yourself. I'm
               going somewhere I can get decent food - not
               staying here with a slut of a wife who can't
               even lift her finger and pull her weight!!!

(*He exits.*)

LAURA

I know where he's gone, I know what he's up to, he's sneaking back to her to get fed and all his washing done. I'll kill him. Well I hope she's cooked him something really disgusting - I hope he chokes on it - I hope he tears it open and little insects scurry out - I hope a big fat slug is hiding in the lettuce. I hope it's infected with bacteria and he vomits in it - I hope it's past its sell-by date and is green with mould - I hope he hates it hates it hates!!!!

(*Spotlight on* KENNETH *downstage.*)

LAURA

Where have you been?

KENNETH

I've been to see Bob.

LAURA

Bob? Bob? Who's Bob?

(*Blackout. Cut to* KENNETH *and* HILARY.)

KENNETH

She does know - she does! I'm putting on weight! It's all those cream cakes you've been feeding me - Christ - I'm done for - how could she suspect? I've been so careful - you haven't been seeing her? No no, you wouldn't - it's just I can't stand her cooking, it makes me feel sick to the stomach. You can understand that can't you?

HILARY

You're a big man - you need a good meal inside you.

KENNETH

Yes, yes! Exactly! Why doesn't she see that - all those burnt offerings - picking at charcoal - pretending it's yummy - I can't stand the farce. I need to be free to eat big meals, wholesome food - it's not that I'm greedy, just hungry - well starving! And her on this diet- it pains me to hear all that calorie counting - skimmed milk, we drink! Can you believe it! I need the thick, creamy, pasteurised kind - grilled chips, we have!

Who ever heard of a grilled chip? I need them sizzling in fat - chunky potatoes - white bread and butter, not crispbread and sunflower margarine - it's obscene!

HILARY   How's your sex life?

KENNETH   What?

HILARY   Your sex life?

KENNETH   Fine.

HILARY   She's nimble and taut - she's still got her waist.

KENNETH   Well yes - I suppose.

HILARY   Well you can't have it both ways, even you must know that.

KENNETH   Why can't she be slim and me be fat? What's the matter with people - all this convention - we don't have to eat the same food . . .

HILARY   It's too tempting for her if she feeds you nice things.

KENNETH   Well, for God's sake - surely she could exercise a little discipline! Is that too much to ask?

HILARY   It was too much for me.

KENNETH   So you got a bit porky, at least I was fed!

HILARY   So why did you spend all your time in her bed?

(*Cut to* LAURA.)

LAURA   I really didn't know I was capable of such thoughts, it's terrible really - the way they creep up on you when you least expect them -

murderous thoughts, cheap and nasty. If only
Hilary would disappear - Ken couldn't find so
much fault with me - no Hilary to compare me
with. If only Hilary wasn't here - Ken would
have to eat my meals - without Hilary we
could be happy - it's just with her still -
around - it makes that hard - a constant
reminder of how good things were, how clean
things were - how well cooked things were -
how well ironed - how neat and how tidy -
how I wish that Hilary would have an
accident - nothing really horrible like a car
crash but maybe roll under something like a
bus - instantly squashed - feeling no pain -
like a rabbit on the road at night - splat - all
over - non-existence - snap my fingers - gone
- not there - "Where's Hilary, I wonder. I
popped round to see her and the place was
deserted". Perhaps she's run off with a
business tycoon - that would serve him right -
but I can't see it happening overnight. I know
it's wrong - God help me, I know - I just can't
help thinking how much easier I'd feel. No
shadowy woman lurking in the past ready to
pounce on me at any minute and tell me what
I've done to her and how happy she made
Ken. I must stop this soon, it leaves a nasty
taste in your mouth - I mean, what's she ever
done to me? I never thought I'd be like this
over a man. I've always thought of myself as
independent and free. It shouldn't matter what
he thinks - I shouldn't let him rule my days -
I'm sorry God for what I said about Hilary -
she deserves a break - it's just I don't think I
can cope with life - being such a useless wife.

(*Lights up on* KENNETH *who is getting dressed
for* HILARY'S *dinner party.*)

KENNETH   You haven't ironed me shirt properly!!!!

LAURA   Sorry - I'll do it again.

KENNETH   It's too late now - shit. Time, Laura - look at the time!!

LAURA   I don't know why we're going.

KENNETH   I've told you - it's rude to turn down invitations. You've got no manners, that's your trouble.

LAURA   I thought we could go to the pictures or stay in.

KENNETH   And what would we eat?!!! Packets of popcorn or one of your messes?!!

LAURA   You could take me out to eat.

KENNETH   I am taking you out to eat.

LAURA   To a restaurant.

KENNETH   And pay good money when I can get fabulous food for free? Anyway, you never eat anything.

LAURA   That's not the point. It's more romantic.

KENNETH   Have you seen my cufflinks?

LAURA   What cufflinks?

KENNETH   You know what cufflinks - I only have one pair.

LAURA   You're not wearing them.

KENNETH   Why not?

LAURA   You know why not.

KENNETH   Just give them to me Laura.

LAURA   No you're just being insensitive - I'm not
            letting you wear something she gave you on
            our anniversary.

KENNETH   You're being childish.

LAURA   I don't think so.

KENNETH   When are you going to start acting like a fully
            grown woman?

LAURA   I don't like being a woman - I don't like it!!!
            I don't like being banished to the kitchen at
            parties talking about stupid things with stupid
            females - I want to be where you are with the
            men all laughing and joking and drinking and
            smoking - I want to join in! I can't do the
            things you ask of me - I'm not like your other
            wife - I'm not cut out for household chores - I
            cannot stand the monotonous, endless
            routines, the mindless activities involved -
            who gives a fuck if the door knobs aren't
            polished?! Why make the bed, just to sleep in
            it again - I can't see the point - it doesn't
            make sense! You do it if you want to - hire
            someone - hire Hilary - anything just to get
            the pressure off my back. I do my best for you
            don't I? It's not like I'm lazy or stupid or
            incompetent - I starve myself for you - I try
            and get my fat bum down and my small tits up
            - I exercise! I know I'm no great cordon bleu
            chef but I have a go - the thanks I get. Have
            you any idea what it feels like to drool over
            cookbooks all day, fantasizing about delicious
            recipes that I'm not allowed to eat in case I
            get fat and even if I could eat them I couldn't
            fucking cook them for the life of me because
            I'm so crap! What happened to me? I was
            young and sexy - you wanted me - now I'm a
            nervous wreck - what have I done - where
            have I gone wrong?

KENNETH   You haven't gone wrong - I have. I should
            never have got a divorce - Hilary would never

have carried on in this screaming, hysterical way - you should be ashamed of yourself. Now get a move on - we'll be late for dinner and you'd better not have a cob on when we get there or there'll be trouble, do you hear me?

(*Blackout.*)

Scene Nine

Rossini's "Barber of Seville" Overture starts up. Back at the dinner scene. LAURA *is a little drunk. All three are now seated.*

LAURA	(*to* HILARY) The bloody times I've had to listen to how great you were, how wonderful - it's hard to imagine he threw you away like a piece of dirt.
KENNETH	Laura, I'll kill you! Just shut your mouth.
LAURA	Did you hear that? He's going to kill me. Me - his wife - the woman he loves.
HILARY	He didn't throw me away actually - I threw him out of my house even though he pleaded with me to stay - isn't that right, Kenneth?
KENNETH	Eh . . . any more of those peanuts?
LAURA	Well, I wish you'd let him stay. I wish you'd stayed together. I wish I'd never set eyes on either of you.
KENNETH	She's been drinking too much - take no notice, she often gets like this. Maybe if she had some food in her stomach, you know?
HILARY	Of course - you must both be famished! It is naughty of me keeping you waiting like this - I hope it's worth it - the famine before the feast!

KENNETH   Oh, of course it will be - it must be ready
now, though. What is it, a slow casserole? Ha!

(KEN *laughs at his joke,* HILARY *laughs
politely but* LAURA *laughs uncontrollably, as
if it's the funniest joke she's ever heard. The
other two stare at her until she stops.*)

HILARY   Patience is a virtue - don't eat any more of
those peanuts. You'll spoil your appetite.
Have an olive instead.

KENNETH   Eh, no thanks - I'll have another drink
though.

LAURA   And I will.

KENNETH   No you won't - you'll sit there and keep
quiet.

HILARY   RIGHT! DINNER IS SERVED!

(HILARY *gets up and stands in the 'kitchen'
area, facing upstage.*)

KENNETH   Thank Christ for that!

LAURA   Don't eat it, Ken. Don't stay here - let's go
home and I'll rustle you up some egg and
chips, you know you like egg and chips.

KENNETH   Not yours I don't.

LAURA   Oh come on, please - we'll go to bed and have
some nookie instead of nosh.

KENNETH   YOU are turning my stomach.

LAURA   But Ken, it's our anniversary! Please come
home with me - I'm your wife. Now.

HILARY   (*enters, carrying tray*) Here it comes!!!

KENNETH	Mmmm - fish for starters - fabulous! Fabulous!!
HILARY	Watch the bones - and eat it slowly - the main course isn't nearly ready.
KENNETH	I just need to get something in me - it looks great Hil - great.
	(KENNETH *mimes eating.* LAURA *and* HILARY *watch him as he gobbles it down like a pig, talking with his mouth full, coughing and spluttering. He has* LAURA'S *fish, too. The more he compliments, the more agitated she becomes. He begins to choke.*)
HILARY	Kenneth - Kenneth! Are you alright?
LAURA	Of course he's not alright - he's choking on a fish bone.
HILARY	Well, shouldn't we do something?
LAURA	Yes, of course - save him.
HILARY	You do it.
LAURA	It's your fish.
HILARY	He can't breathe.
LAURA	I know.
HILARY	He wants a drink.
	(LAURA *drains her glass.*)
LAURA	Mine's all gone.
HILARY	He should try and cough it up.
LAURA	He should just give in - he's spitting everywhere.

HILARY	Kenneth - just swallow hard.
LAURA	That's made it worse.
HILARY	I can't bear to look.
LAURA	No, neither can I.

(They hide their faces in their hands and look away. KEN has several moments of fighting for air until he eventually has an attack of convulsions, his body jerking viciously on the table before he collapses. Dead. There is silence. The women slowly look towards his body. The reflect quietly, concerned and shocked.)

LAURA	We've done it now, you know.
HILARY	We've had it.
LAURA	We have.
HILARY	We've done it.
LAURA	We have.
HILARY	We're really gonna be in for it - I mean he was a very good husband.
LAURA	He was.
HILARY	He was respectable enough.
LAURA	He was.
HILARY	He never lifted a finger to me in all those years and I've heard some terrible stories about violent men, murdering men, drunks and pigs and child abusers, wife batterers and overbearing bastards and I've pitied those women - the women married to men like that should have the world's sympathy - but who ever felt sorry for me? All the years he was

with me he was decent and responsible - he
paid the mortgage - made decisions and he
NEVER LIFTED A FINGER! Well, hoo-
fucking-rah! Big deal! Should we throw a
party and celebrate, count our blessings and
forgo our happiness because we happened to
pick one that controlled his temper!? I wanted
to feel more than lucky and relieved - I
wanted to feel danger and excitement and
opportunity, too - not live a life where the
best I can say is there's nothing to complain
about! We count ourselves lucky cause there's
always someone worse off than us and our life
goes by then we wake up and realise too late
that it didn't have to be like that - suddenly
you see things you could have done - the
person you could have been - why should he
have all the fun?

LAURA   So why did you get married?

HILARY   It was the logical conclusion to being in love
- or so we were told, and we listened to
voices in those days. We never asked who
they belonged to.

LAURA   I mean if he had been one of those men, those
violent nasty men - if he'd tormented you and
battered you and threatened to kill you, you
still couldn't kill him - I mean they'd put you
away for twenty five years - so you can't kill
your husband just because he left you.

HILARY   You can't kill your husband just because he
undermined you.

LAURA   You can't kill your husband just because he
was boring.

HILARY   And fat.

LAURA   And greedy.

HILARY   And held you back.

LAURA   And ageing.

HILARY   Because you felt like it.

LAURA   Let's face it, you can't kill your husband!

HILARY   But we have.

LAURA   I know.

HILARY   They'll make an example of us, that's for sure.

LAURA   Bring back hanging just for us.

HILARY   I suppose they're frightened it'll start a growing trend.

LAURA   In husband murdering? Yes! Of course!

HILARY   It's not fair is it? You can kill your wife if she leaves you.

LAURA   You can kill your wife if she nags you.

HILARY   You can kill your wife if she looks the wrong way.

LAURA   At the drop of fucking hat!

HILARY   Do you think they'll hold us up as a disgrace to womankind?

LAURA   Well, it's not the sort of thing we're meant to do, is it?

HILARY   Do you think we're evil?

LAURA   I don't feel evil.

HILARY   Neither do I.

LAURA   Perhaps we're mad.

HILARY   They'll call us witches.

LAURA   And burn us or duck us.

HILARY   We're widows now.

LAURA   Unmarried - uncontrolled.

HILARY   Even if they don't hang us they'll find us men
              to keep an eye on us.

LAURA   Well, we'll have to get rid of the body.

HILARY   Dispose of it - lose it - disappear it - leaving
              no trace.

LAURA   How? He's a big man.

HILARY   Not if we cut him up.

LAURA   We couldn't!! Then what do we do?

HILARY   Turn on the oven - 400°F.

LAURA   We can't! Well, you'll have to do it - I'm a
              terrible cook.

HILARY   What do we do once we've cooked him?

LAURA   Well, I don't know.

HILARY   He's your husband.

LAURA   You saw him first!

HILARY   We'll have to eat him.

LAURA   I'm on a diet!!!!

HILARY   It's the only safe way to dispose of the body -
              eat him then take a few laxatives. Either way
              - as long as he's flushed down the loo.

LAURA   He'd kill us if he knew.

HILARY   Well, he doesn't - so - you must be hungry by
                 now.

LAURA   Well I suppose a little peckish - what were we
                 having for dinner?

HILARY   I told you - a surprise!

LAURA   Oh . . . yeah.

                 (*Music: "Glory Glory" from Elvis's "An
                 American Trilogy". The music has slowly
                 been rising towards the end of the scene - now
                 it blasts out as* LAURA *and* HILARY *toast with
                 their glasses and look at each other, they
                 slide down in their huge chairs and smile
                 triumphantly. A freeze as the lighting changes
                 and the music reaches a crescendo. Blackout.*)